TRAVELING TED'S

POSTCARDS

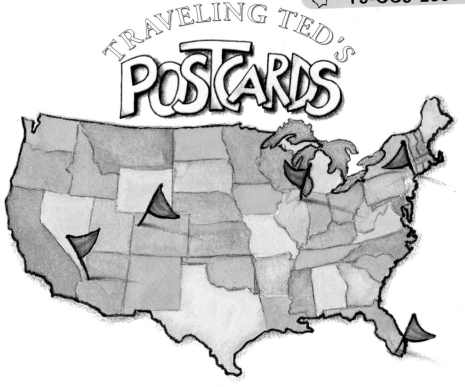

Written by Andrea Butler
Illustrated by Maureen Fisher Rivkin

CelebrationPress

An Imprint of ScottForesman
A Division of HarperCollins*Publishers*

Traveling Ted went on a trip.

2

April 2

Dear Friends,
    Today I saw the
Statue of Liberty. It
was big.

Love,
Ted

Mrs. Ortega's Class
Playhouse School
Los Angeles, CA
90024

He went on a plane.

April 3

Dear Friends,
    Today I went on a
little boat. I saw an
alligator.
                    Love,
                    Ted

Mrs. Ortega's Class
Playhouse School
Los Angeles, CA
90024

He went on a boat.

Dear Friends,
    Today I went to the zoo. I liked the giraffe best.

April 4

Love,
Ted

Mrs. Ortega's Class
Playhouse School
Los Angeles, CA
90024

He went on a bus.

April 5

Dear Friends,
Today I went down into the Grand Canyon on a donkey. It was scary.

Love,
Ted

Mrs. Ortega's Class
Playhouse School
Los Angeles, CA
90024

He went on a donkey.

April 6

Dear Friends,
    Today I went up in the mountains. It was cold.

Love,
Ted

Mrs. Ortega's Class
Playhouse School
Los Angeles, CA
90024

25¢

He went on a train.

Then he came home.